Food for Life

PRAIRIES

KATE RIGGS

Published by Creative Education
P.O. Box 227, Mankato, Minnesota 56002
Creative Education is an imprint of The Creative Company
www.thecreativecompany.us

Design and production by Liddy Walseth
Art direction by Rita Marshall
Printed in the United States of America

Photographs by Alamy (Don Johnston), Corbis (W. Perry Conway, David
Muench, Richard Hamilton Smith), Getty Images (James Balog, Peter
Dennen, Jerry Dodrill, Tim Fitzharris, James Hager, Frank Krahmer, Frank
Oberle, Norbert Rosing, Phil Schermeister, Tom Walker, Konrad Wothe),
Minden Pictures (Piotr Naskrecki)

Library of Congress Cataloging-in-Publication Data
Riggs, Kate.
Prairies / by Kate Riggs.
p. cm. — (Food for life)
Includes index.
Summary: A fundamental look at a common food chain on the prairie,
starting with the widespread bluestem grass, ending with the badger, and
introducing various animals in between.
ISBN 978-1-58341-830-7
1. Prairie ecology—Juvenile literature. 2. Food chains (Ecology)—
Juvenile literature.
I. Title. II. Series.

QH541.5.P7R53 2010
577.4'416—dc22 2009004783

First Edition
2 4 6 8 9 7 5 3 1

Food for Life
PRAIRIES

KATE RIGGS

A GREEN BOOK

A food chain shows what living things in an area eat. Plants are the first link on a food chain. Animals that eat plants or other animals make up the rest of the links.

A prairie is a large, grassy area. The land is mostly flat. There are not many trees. The soil underneath the grass is good for growing crops.

THE MAIN *PREDATORS* OF PLANT-EATING PRAIRIE DOGS ARE HAWKS, BADGERS, AND COYOTES.

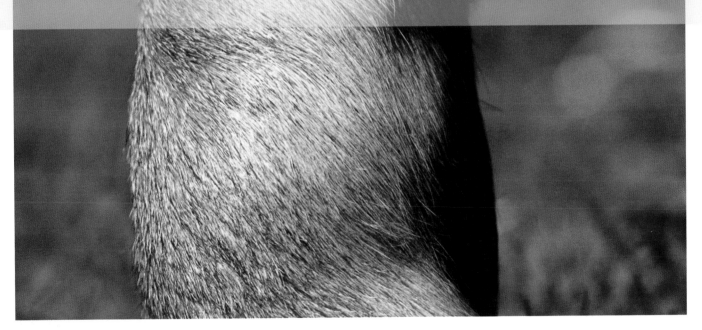

LOTS OF BUFFALO USED TO
THE UNITED STATES IN HUGE

LIVE ON THE PRAIRIES OF GROUPS CALLED HERDS.

Grass grows well on the prairie, too. A grass called bluestem can grow to be 10 feet (3 m) tall! Bluestem is nicknamed "turkey foot grass." The tips of the grass look like the birds' feet.

Grasshoppers are bugs that live on the prairie. They eat bluestem grass. Grasshoppers use their long _antennae_ (an-TEN-eye) to find good grass to eat. They use their strong mouths to chomp through the grass.

The prairie shrew eats grasshoppers. Shrews are mouselike animals that make their nests in the tall bluestem grass. They are _territorial_. They do not like to share their nests or their food.

RED-TAILED HAWKS EAT
ANIMALS. THEY HAVE

SNAKES AND OTHER PRAIRIE
A SCREAMING CRY.

Bull snakes use their forked tongues to smell for _prey_. When it smells a shrew, the snake attacks it. It wraps itself around the shrew so the animal cannot get away.

Badgers are not afraid of
bull snakes. They like to eat
snakes. Badgers have long
claws that are good for digging.
They dig for snakes that
are hiding underground.

PRAIRIES IN AFRICA SAVANNAS. ZEBRAS AND

ARE CALLED VELDS AND ELEPHANTS EAT THE GRASSES.

All of these living things make up a food chain. The bluestem grass grows on the prairie. The grasshopper eats the bluestem. The prairie shrew eats the grasshopper. The bull snake eats the shrew. And the badger eats the bull snake.

PRAIRIE EARTHWORMS EAT DEAD GRASS. THEY HELP PUT _NUTRIENTS_ BACK INTO THE GROUND.

Some day, the badger will die. Its body will break down into nutrients (NOO-tree-ents). These nutrients will go into the ground and help plants such as the bluestem grass grow. Then the prairie food chain will start all over again.

READ MORE ABOUT IT

Fleisher, Paul. *Grassland Food Webs*. Minneapolis: Lerner Publications, 2008.

Kalman, Bobbie, and Kelley MacAulay. *Prairie Food Chains*. New York: Crabtree Publishing Company, 2006.

GLOSSARY

antennae—long, thin feelers that are on top of a bug's head

nutrients—things in soil and food that help plants and animals grow strong and healthy

predators—animals that kill and eat other animals

prey—an animal that is eaten by another animal

territorial—behaving in ways to protect a home area

INDEX